Complete.
Done.
Finished.

The joy of doing,
the freedom when done

Martha Ringer

MARTHA'S TREATS
COLLECTION
martharinger.com

Published by Martha Ringer
www.martharinger.com

Printed in United States of America

ISBN: 978-0-615-19417-2

Library of Congress Control Number: 2008903218

Original Watercolors by
Martha Ringer

Book Design by Shelley Noble
Author Photo by Art Durand

Acknowledgments

I bless every person who has been on this book journey with me.

I honor my dearest friend, Bea Young, who was my champion throughout. Everyone should have a Bea in their lives who believes in them 100%.

Thank you with love to my creative advisors: Leigh Briggin, Christine Godwin, Susan Gravel, Katie Hendricks, Eva Lier, Rose Michael, Pryor Nunn, Scott Ringer, and Joe Zazzu.

I deeply appreciate my editors: Pat Moore, Nann Kyra, and Mary Vaessen.

Thank you David Allen, Kathryn Allen, and Dean Acheson for starting me in this work. And thank you to all my clients from whom I receive great blessings.

My deepest gratitude is to my Beloved wayshowers, John-Roger and John Morton, and to Spirit, who truly wrote this book.

To the Spirit
that is you and me

Introduction

I have spent my life learning how to be present in my doing, and I am still learning. I have discovered "doing" to just get it done is not the most satisfying way to work. Reading 100 books in grammar school for the summer library reading program was not about enjoyment along the way, it was a race to the finish to win.

Now I am seeing completing as a sacred art: a way to stay conscious and present in my being as I get things done and to experience the pleasure and enjoyment of doing.

This book is intended to look at the value of completing, the joy that is part of finishing something with focus and intention, so that doing becomes a natural extension of loving versus a push (without mercy) to the end.

I believe we are here to finish our loose ends so we can go back home to God. Engaging our own cooperation and staying with ourselves through to completion is the secret and the blessing.

Contents

Middle... *Practical Actions*

End... *Taking the first step*

Everything that has a
beginning has an ending.
Make peace with that
and all will be well.

Buddha

Beginning...

Back full circle

Back full circle to the beginning is what completing is about. You keep getting to start, over and over, at the beginning until it is done.

The beginning is wherever you are. You start where you are. If you have a backlog of incompletes, you start there.

Completing is about conscious choices. If we proceed against what is not aligned, we impede the completing process.

If you choose to begin something, also choose to complete it. We are responsible for what we put in motion until we declare it complete.

Complete only
what is yours to do

2

Gathering ourselves here to now

Declare complete all those things you never remember even agreeing to do. Repeat out loud: "Everything I have ever said I would do and did not do, I now declare complete."

Have you considered that many of your incompletions are unexpressed wishes? If you had dreams in the past that were not complete, it is a good idea to acknowledge them, write them down, and declare them complete if you no longer choose to do them.

Continually choose what is now to do. Complete what is yours to do. For me this book has been on my plate for six years. It has had many phases. Finally, I realized I had to relax and allow it to be completed in its own time. At some point you must either finish it or declare it complete. I chose to finish this one.

4

Simple ingredients to completing

Completing has very simple ingredients: a daily, consistent habit of processing what comes in, cooperation, making only agreements you intend to keep, appreciating and rewarding, and, the most important, moving, acting, doing, and participating.

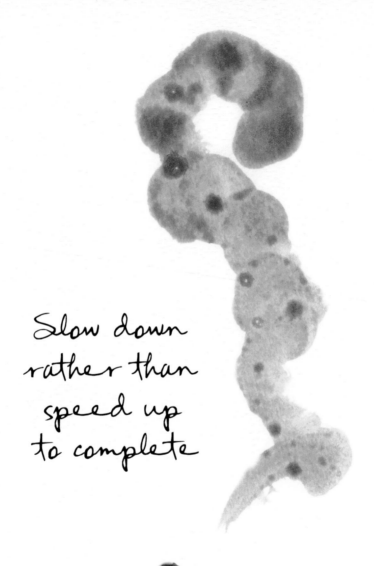

Slow down
rather than
speed up
to complete

Slowing down to now

When I get ahead of myself, all I need to do is focus on finishing one thing at a time by beginning to move ever so slowly...so the doing can connect up with my being.

Focus is giving yourself the
opportunity to be present to
what most needs your attention

Relaxing into focus

Most people do not think about relaxing to get to a place of focus. I have discovered that relaxing is how I can focus. If I want to see a word on the page that looks a little fuzzy, squinting to see it makes it more difficult to see. Relaxing the eye brings the word into clearer view. If I want to figure something out, I can pull my forehead together and create those lines above the nose or expand my vision by widening my eyes and see with awe and wonder as I find a solution. Relaxing and expanding brings the clarity.

10

Patience as a practice

Let's practice patience.

Let's stay with the letter we are writing until it is complete before we write the next one.

We cannot type or write two letters at once, just like we cannot handle two pieces of paper at once…it is first one, then the other.

We cannot walk by moving both feet at the same time…it's one foot then the other foot, then back to the first foot.

It's a divine design to keep us focused on *one at a time.*

We cannot speak two words at the same time. It's one word after the next as soon as a word is completed.

If we follow the divine design laid out for us—using one letter, one word, or one foot at a time—we walk in patient peace.

12

Immersion in the moment

Completing is a process of 100 percent immersion into the action, otherwise something is still missing. With my full being present, the action gets completed all the way, without the dangling participle of a sentence that has no home. I think that is at the crux of the cap on/off the toothpaste. We leave in our consciousness before we are done because we are rushing off to the next thing. When I let myself be fully in the writing of a note, my penmanship is clear.

If I am present with myself, my life completes as I go in perfect timing moments. I hear clearly what to do, the person I need to talk to calls me, and I walk through my day in freedom.

Honor yourself
by choosing to finish

Choosing to complete

"I am going to go now" is the choice to complete the conversation.

"I am going to let you go" is a way not to choose to complete the conversation.

"I am choosing to complete this project" expresses you are taking responsibility for doing it.

"I have to complete this project" is a statement of being a victim.

Complete your actions with choice. Thinking or feeling that you *have to* or *should* takes the joy out of doing.

In the choosing is the freedom.

Listening for the next move

The quietness in my consciousness is louder than my mind chatter. I stop and wait for the next line to be delivered, trusting it will always come. Each day is like a surprise delivery of the unexpected if I choose to receive it that way. When I ask my clients to write down their intention for our session together, *more space* is what so many of them write. Space opens when I listen with expansion. No need to rush. A slow pace creates all the space in the world. Complete from that state of consciousness. That is the ultimate freedom… relaxing while doing. We can trust we will be given what is next if we simply pay attention. The willingness to listen first (before taking action) is the key to successful completing.

All ideas don't need
to be completed,
just acknowledged
by writing them down

Leaving nothing to memory

The best way I know to get myself present in the moment is to start writing down what is in my head (literally). If I have lots of ideas showing up about future projects, I write those down. If I have things to do, I write those down. If I have none of those, I simply write what is in my heart to say. And, I do it until I am empty.

To me the practice of writing things down is an honoring of myself and what is going on. If I am angry, writing it down (then burning the paper and letting it go) acknowledges the anger versus stuffing it away and pretending it is not there. If I am grateful, writing it down makes more gratitude. If I have things to do, then I let my mind go off duty and relax and I take responsibility for the completing.

Writing things down for me is staying clear as I go.

The flow of completing leads
gracefully from one thing
to the next

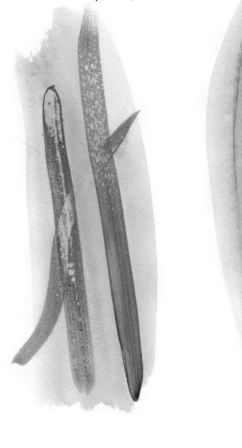

Flowing one step to the next

Stay on track inside, and the outside will move into alignment in your support. Receive what is next as the gift that it is. God always gives us the next line. If you start speeding up, reverse into slow gear and experience how the relaxing creates more ease in your doing. If you find yourself stuck in trying to explain and figure things out, stop and breathe. The interconnectedness and the why-fors and the how-comes are not as important. While fun to share, the explanations of how it all took place take us out of the present moment. If we stay with the essence of what needs communicating, we create greater flow to our doing. When we are in the flow, we are shown the clear direction to what is next.

Taste the sweetness of
completing down to the truth

Telling the heart's truth

All of the times we don't say what our heart wants to say, we are incomplete. Telling the heart's truth in the moment keeps us alive and current. The unspoken gets to speak and be heard, and we relax as nothing is holding us back.

Loving is completing

Without interrupting yourself

Take interruptions without interrupting yourself. Consciously choose to stop doing something before you start something else. In caring for a child, the recommended technique these days is to tell a child when you are going to pick them up so you don't yank them away from the moment for your own convenience.

We would never dream of letting go of an infant in our arms to answer the doorbell, yet we are willing to yank ourselves away from our own attention 100 times a day or more, allowing our own or others' interruptions.

Watch where your attention goes
and ask if you are to follow

Quieting the mind to the infinitesimal second

Completing is an inner process carried out physically. The inner part is the conscious awareness of and connection to our own attention. As we take the action, it requires quieting the mind to the infinitesimal second and holding the focus through to the next second.

I experience this when I write on paper and slow down the movement of my pen until I can follow each letter as it is formed through to completion. What I notice happens immediately is I come present with the pen as it moves, my body relaxes, I feel like I have access to universes of information, and my mind quiets down and effortlessly receives what is delivered.

The ultimate act of loving

Can we love ourselves enough to finish a thought and let others finish their thoughts? I hadn't considered that every time I interrupt someone's thoughts, I am possibly responsible for the incompletion of theirs that I left dangling.

Sometimes it seems that if we just hold on to our thoughts all will be well. In fact, our thoughts are like a stream that is ongoing and meant to continue that way. We want to let them come in and then let them go and then get right back to the moment at hand. Sometimes a thought will be something to act on and then we choose to act.

Declare your own loving for yourself by writing down your thinking and then deciding if there is any energy to match it into action.

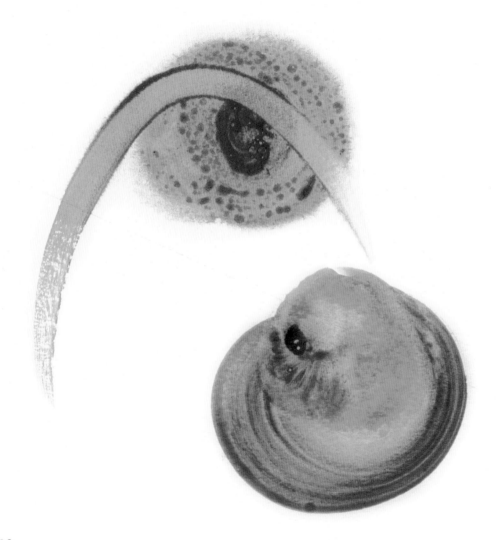

30

Complete thee this day

Do you unconsciously carry over yesterday's leftovers into today?

Beginning and ending your day with intention can make the completing process quite simple.

Appreciate what you completed.

Look ahead to the next day, and place your attention on where you want to commit yourself.

I shudder when I look
at all the clutter
Let's go have tea with
scones & butter
I'm not ready to clean up this mess
I'd rather drink tea in
my new yellow dress

What's on track

The discipline to do what needs doing will lead to freedom. Accurately listening to the intuition to follow the timing of what is next makes the process flow.

Sometimes scones and butter are the most on track thing to do.

What is clear to do is always revealed with patience and a listening heart.

The unspoken
statement behind
"I want to get organized"
is "I want to be able
to find and use
what I have"

Using what is given

A friend once asked me if I thought I was compulsive in how I keep my home. I honestly looked at it, since there was a time when I would have agreed with her. What I have grown to appreciate is the peace of having only what I use and having it located where it is accessible to use.

Maybe usability is a more appropriate word for organizing. The simplicity of reaching for something and having it within seconds is freeing and allows us to use our attention and focus for creating and not for searching.

Forgiving blesses all
the incompletes

Forgiving – the absolute completer

So what do you do with all the things you know you didn't finish and that you can't go back and complete? Declare them done, and let them go. Bless the experience for what it taught you, and declare finished the burden of carrying around the judgment one second longer.

Forgiving our judgments against ourselves is the key to completing. When you make a judgment against yourself or against someone else, there is a simple way to handle it in the moment. It sounds like this:

I forgive myself for judging myself for forgetting to do X.

I forgive myself for judging myself as incompetent for not catching that error in the document.

I forgive myself for judging myself for gossiping about my boss.

If we truly forgive ourselves, the judgment will not appear in your mind again. Practice forgiveness so you are always complete and up to date.

Now is the divine action

Middle...

Completing is the way
I count on myself

Commitment

More important than all the tools and actions needed for completing is the first step...commitment.

Completing requires an attitude of no-matter-what-I-will.

And in that willingness is the grace to complete.

Before I work with a client, I ask for their commitment to learning what they might need to learn about completing so there is a foundation for completing before we begin.

If you want a completing focus in your life, say out loud now: I commit to learning whatever I need to learn to live in a continual flow of completing.

Completing has little to
do with organizing and
everything to do with
moving, acting, and doing

The way into action is a single step

Doing is a step-by-step process. Completing is a continuing of the steps one after another until something is finished. When we are in the flow of doing, moving along step-by-step is quite easy. When we procrastinate to begin, we need a way into the beginning. On the second day of a session, I give my clients time to work. I observe them hesitate to choose an action. I watch them think, look over the list a few times, and think some more until I intervene, suggesting they simply pick anything on the list and do it. It's all about moving and doing and not thinking.

Choosing, moving, and doing are keys to completing. It starts with figuring out the next action step right up front (this is the "thinking" part). The definition of a next action step is something you can physically do in one step. The physical part of the definition is the key. When someone is stuck trying to analyze and think what to do, I simply suggest they move physically and start doing it so the next action becomes clear. Doing stays alive if we keep doing the next physical action step.

Quiet the urgency

What is all the urgency?

We have forgotten our experience of knowing that what we need to handle is given to us in perfect timing. We have added a layer on top that looks and sounds like urgency; rushing for a cell phone call with a kind of intensity that seems as if missing this call would be a catastrophe; jumping to answer the office phone as if what we are doing is less important, forgetting to check with ourselves to see what is most on purpose; rushing with our bodies by walking with intensity and speed; speaking quickly as if we can't get our words out fast enough. What is our hurry? What is the urgency that pushes us out of the moment of knowing? What if we all just stopped for a moment, took a breath, and relaxed into our own focus where we know what is on purpose for us to do. Give yourself time to connect to your inner director of action, letting go of the urgency to react to outer stimuli.

Our attention
is distracted by our
incomplete actions being
held in our head

Write it down

All the things we tell ourselves and others we will do represent agreements we make with ourselves.

Keeping agreements is essential to our well being. The simplest way to keep agreements is to not make any we know we can't keep and to keep the ones we do make.

The only way to track your agreements is to write them down. I refuse to keep anything in my head. It is, we are, too precious for that.

The price we pay for not keeping our agreements is visible: fatigue, confusion, irritability, low self-esteem, lack of trust.

If we do what we say we will do, we get the goodies of energy, clarity, focus, and the most valuable goodie…self trust and the trust of others.

Trust yourself to do what you say you will do.

Space for creative completing

In our world, quiet uninterrupted space is a luxury. Choosing time and space for inner attunement to our creative spirit brings in the information that might otherwise be missed. Watch out for over-scheduling on your calendar. Give yourself empty space for "simply being." It's not so much the amount of time, but the commitment to making yourself important enough to have that space and valuing and appreciating that time alone. For me, "simply being" is a way of relaxing my focus with walking breaks outside, drawing or doodling on paper either with pen or paintbrush—no goal, no reason, just time to let myself play for a little while and see what emerges. When I am "simply being," I find I am given the keys to creatively complete things in my life in ways I might not otherwise have imagined. I also find whatever I do after my "simply being" moments is more fun and even more inspired.

Consciously choose each action

One thing at a time

Completing is a "being" action focusing our full undivided attention on one thing at a time. Immersing ourselves in the moment is the way to finish relaxed.

Place your attention heart-fully. Choose where you want your focus to be each moment.

We keep thinking if we do a lot of things simultaneously, we will get to the finish line more quickly. It is not true.

Some of my clients insist on using the monthly calendar view on their screen. I watch their clarity come into focus when they switch their calendar screen to the day view.

Imagine asking a child to effectively deal with today while giving him his whole schedule for the month.

Our consciousness is begging our cooperation to stay present here and now no matter what we think.

Day by day

My calendar is one of my most trusted assistants. I start my day looking at my calendar (not my in-box), and I end my day looking at my calendar so I can see what took place, what I still need to complete, and what is coming up tomorrow. I can relax, knowing I can count on myself to look and be prepared for what is showing up. My calendar lets me relax into focus. I can easily track what is happening and can schedule time I have available to complete actions.

Withhold no more

How do you tell your heart's truth?

What we withhold, both from ourselves and from other people, takes a great deal of attention that is often unconscious. If we dare to tell people what is true for us—honestly, without an agenda, straight from the heart—we are free. If you see something that could assist someone, you can ask them if you can give them feedback. If they say no, you respect their decision. If you see a creative solution at work, offer it to the one who can do something about it. Do it without an expectation or without blaming them in any way for the way it is now. Simply offer your creativity and awareness. If you are angry with a spouse, or with a boss, tell them what is going on (without the anger). Together you can bring balance to the situation and let the anger be released without dumping it on someone or yourself (by keeping it inside). Imagine the freed-up energy that could be released if we were willing to tell our heart's truth with loving.

Focusing

Focusing our attention is the place where completing happens. When I am in the moment with my full attention, I can do more in one minute than it might take me an hour to do if I let myself be distracted.

Interruptions take away your attention.

Try seeing if you can hold your mind empty for even ten seconds without a thought. Not so easy. True focus is the ability to stay present in the moment with your undivided attention on only one thing. Letting cell phones, email message alerts, or drive-bys* interrupt us is a choice. Make a choice to focus on completing, and let go of the distractions.

*Drive-bys are people popping into your office for a quick answer they didn't feel like putting in writing.

Acknowledgment

When was the last time you said out loud to yourself, "Good job X *(your name)*?" We more easily say that to others or to our dogs. The incentive to start the next thing starts with acknowledging the last thing we completed. If you want to truly live an active life of completing, reward yourself every time you finish something with an out-loud acknowledgment from you to you. We all were given encouragement, attention, and acknowledgment as we learned to walk and talk. We need the same acknowledgment as we continue to learn new things. For many of us, completing is something new to learn.

Awareness is the
willingness to look and see

Looking

A willingness to look at what is not done is all it takes to get our full attention present in the moment. Wondering, worrying, thinking about it doesn't do a thing. Simply looking at what is on lists of actions and projects that need completing, lets you relax as the lists tell the truth. The reality is that it usually is not as bad as the imagination thinks. Often my clients believe they have far more to do than the final lists actually show. When they see it all in writing in front of them, they calm down. We just have to keep looking at the pictures (lists and papers) to be conscious and aware and keep ourselves on track.

The key to completing is
moving into action, picking
up one thing at a time
& taking a next step

Start where you are

We are highly creative beings. Sometimes we over-create and over-commit, resulting in many incompletions. Changing a lifetime of not completing takes a willingness and commitment to begin.

Start paying attention. Notice when you stop in the middle of a sentence and don't finish a thought, when you leave a conversation and let your mind wander, when you jump in and finish other peoples' sentences, and when you don't write down something you just said you would do. What do you do when you notice it? At first, do only that. Start being aware of the incompletes in your life. When you become more conscious of your incompletions, you will start to change.

The first step is to write down everything you know of that you said you would do or would like to do. Figure out your next action steps, and do them or put them on a list. You don't have to do it perfectly. You just have to start. From now on in your life, start writing down, in one place, what you agree to do.

Always laughter and joy

We must make it fun. Fill your doing and completing with as much joy and laughter as you can. For me there is great freedom in joy and laughter. A year ago one of my clients said the only way she can deal with her in-box is to pretend each thing is a big surprise she is receiving. If you set up Outlook (or most email programs now) to open the next email immediately upon deleting or moving the previous email to a file, you will always have the surprise factor. Read your email with relaxed eyes and shoulders. See what you are reading with wonder instead of judgment about what is being sent or the person sending it. If you keep your attention on defining next action steps, you will take the emotional reactive part of your consciousness out of the equation. Then it is just information and action. Giggling at what you receive is one way to neutralize any reactiveness you might have.

The end is just
the beginning

End...

Endings lead right into beginnings

Endings are usually over with quite quickly—the last word in a conversation, the last word typed in a memo, the last word in a book. And as soon as you come to the end, you begin again.

You have come to the end of my part of this book. You are Complete. Done. Finished. with reading. Now it is your turn to begin with your first step in completing.

I acknowledge you and thank you for choosing this book and for choosing to make focusing and completing important in your life.

Please turn the page...

Start everything
with willingness,
and cooperation
steps right in

Your first step

What gets us to take the first step? If you declared the commitment statement out loud *(page 41)*, then that part is handled. The next step is to simply start moving. So stand up right now, holding this book open to this page.

Notice just that little step of standing moved you into action. Now take another step. Ask yourself what is one thing you could complete for yourself that would bring you joy? Make it something you can do within one day. Write it down right now on the line below.

I will _____

_____

_____

Now turn the page for your next steps...

Now back to
the beginning

Begin right now

Here are your instructions:

1. Start right now and complete what you wrote down. If that is not possible due to time, schedule it for the next day or two.

2. Then, when that item is **Complete. Done. Finished.** go to martharinger.com and enter it in the "*Celebrate Completing!*" box and click "Next Step." Continue to celebrate yourself every day for the things you complete. Feel free to enter them on martharinger.com in the "Celebrate Completing!" box as often as you like.

3. Now, take one step or idea you liked while reading this book, such as writing down agreements, and do it consistently for 32 days in a row. If you miss a day, start the count over at one until you have 32 days of doing a new behavior consistently. That creates a new habit.

Next steps

First-Steps-First *(consulting sessions)*

If you loved this book, you will love the freedom and joy that come from two days of working one-on-one with Martha, experiencing the power of focusing your undivided attention on completing. Finishing a significant number of your own "incompletes" during the two days, while learning how to both work effectively and use a system customized for you to keep current with your work, is life changing. Invest in establishing greater focused attention and making completing a way of life.

*For more information, email martha@**martharinger.com***

Martha Treats *(monthly eNewsletter)*

Martha Treats are inspirational pieces written to support clients and subscribers as they focus on completing.

*Subscribe for FREE on **martharinger.com***

Martha Invites *(blog)*

You are invited to exchange experiences of focusing and completing here. Readers and clients are encouraged to participate in the fun. It is updated often.

*Join the conversation on **martharinger.com***

Martha's Treats Collection

Loving Who You Are – *The essence of completing*
(spoken word and soothing music CD) *$14.95*

Motivating, inspiring, comforting, and clear. Martha's words are unscripted and spoken from the heart. Martha's voice is intimate, conversational, and genuine. She makes the action of completing simple, fun, and hopeful. People are listening again and again, inspired and trusting there is joy in completing and living in the present moment. Great for commuting and bedtime relaxation for you or your loved ones. (60 minutes)

Available at Martha's Treats Collection on **martharinger.com**

Complete. Done. Finished.– *The joy of doing, the freedom when done* *(hardcover gift book)* *$24.95*

Completing is all about moving and doing. Martha illustrates the joy of moving and doing with her own spontaneous brush strokes that highlight the wisdom of her words. You will be immersed in the delight of completing as you read this book, and you will be inspired to act. Martha has a gift for communicating what she has experienced and knows with her heart. (full color)

Available at Martha's Treats Collection on **martharinger.com**